My Write to Heal

Keelia Trively

To my little sister, Kelly.
You are my whole heart and my whole world.
You are my 'why.'

A Note of Caution

A note of caution to all who enter.

These pages are a minefield in which I want you to feel comfortable walking around aimlessly.

These words are simply truths that have transpired in my own life up to this very moment in time where you find yourself reading them.

This is my past,

And I know it's many of your pasts, too.

I will not apologize.

Neither should you.

Let these pages show you you're not alone.

Let all the emotions you feel as you read rise up,

And out,

Of you so you can let go of this past,

Of your past,

And grab hold of your sweet future.

the Poems

Once Upon a Time	6
Heart of the Story	7
I Am From	12
Colors of Pain	16
All That Is Mine	19
Dear World	26
It Rained Last Night	33
Dear Quiet Renaissance Man	37
My Giant	42
Dear Fear	46
The End	49

Once Upon a Time

Once upon a time,
In a land far away,
In a time long ago,
In a castle above the trees.

This is the story of a girl who lost her shoe.
This is the story of a girl who ate an apple.
This is the story of a girl who loved her father.

This is a fairy tale.

How many of these tales have I lived through?
How many have broken my heart and made me think,
The perfect soul does indeed exist?
How many times have I been lied to by ink
      and paper?

Heart of the Story

Is it wrong to want the heart of this story to be me?

I want these poems to be me in writing.

My life,

What I have lived so far,

Outlined and traced in the pages of an object that has filled my soul with such comfort over the years.

I want to offer this part of me to anyone willing to open these white pages and peer into their contents.

I want to enfold my truths,

And my traumas,

Into this binding.

Not so I can re-live them.

But so I can finally be free of them.

So I can let them escape me.

Give them some other place to reside in,

That isn't in me.

I want to free myself of these bonds from
     my past.
And allow myself to be swept away with
     my future.

That isn't too much to ask.
And I'm not going to ask for permission.
It's my life.
It's my truths.
I can share them and move them wherever
     I please.
And it'll please me,
And pain me,
To move them out of myself and onto these pages
     I have starred at for hours.
Being so afraid of their possibilities that
     almost nothing came of them.

Does that make me feel guilty?
Yes,
I won't lie to you.
But that's why I know it's okay.
After all,
I'm only human.

No matter how much I try to be more than that,
I am only human.
Soft.
Fragile.
Explosive.

I once read a quote saying,
"A woman may be delicate,
But she isn't delicate like a flower.
No.
She is delicate,
Like a bomb."
That's what I want to be.

So let these words be explosive.
Let them leap off this page and shatter your world until you see your own truths.
Let this binding be strewn across the floor once you finish reading,
Reminding you to un-glue your own life so you can create everything your diminished heart has ever desired.
Let these pages propel you into the next chapter of your life.

Not knowing how it'll start,
Or how it'll end.
Just excited to see what is possible.

Do you understand the immense possibilities
    within each blank page and empty notebook?
Entire worlds have been,
And are being,
Created and destroyed.
Truths that shake all of humanity,
Written for us to consume.

The knowledge that most are too afraid,
Or too stubborn,
To accept.

This isn't just in books written on the real
    world.
Fantasy has as much truth as a textbook,
If you read close enough.

Words that come to life and shape how the
    real world exists.
It's the closest anyone can get to playing god.
Creating and destroying life with just
    one breath.
Just one stroke of a pen or keyboard.

Does that scare you?
Or liberate you?
Let it shatter your caged world and set you free,
My friend.
We need your truths to be free.
We need you,
To be free.

I am from the place my parents did not grow up,

To lost moving vans and old pictures wrapped in newspaper.

I'm from the dream of a red front door and a wrap-around porch,

To too many scream-filled nights.

I'm from the blossoming of a flower I willed to bloom under the concrete of my skin.

To the long rains and loud thunderstorms that lulled me to sleep.

I'm from the risks I was forced to take and the loves I was forced to hate.

I'm from dance recitals and empty glitter bottles,

To Twizzler packages because we couldn't eat nachos in our costumes.

I'm from sisters and brothers and the only thing we don't share is blood.

I'm from long nights and lonely mornings and there's no time for breakfast.

I'm from wishing I had time to rest and loving those days I never sit down.

I'm from learning from a science textbook to
    living from the word of God.
I'm from the land "Where The Wild Things Are,"
And hearing my mother tell me
    "I'll love you forever."
Yet not really believing her.

Cinderella was my girl and I've always loved
    glass slippers.
But there's that voice in my head telling me
    those are impractical.
I'm from always be yourself but no matter
    what you'll never be good enough.
So what should I be?

Society tells me there's something wrong with me.
God tells me I'm worth dying for.

I'm from confusion and love and the only emotion
    we seem to grasp today is hate.
I'm from airports that see more love than
    churches and back alleys that see more
    death than morticians.

I'm from countries I can't pronounce and not the resort side of that place.

I'm from a child's laughter and a mother's love,

As she gives her last piece of food away.

I'm from begging and asking for money on the streets,

Because our world doesn't take care of those who fight for us.

I'm from sunsets and sunrises,

And singing praises to God under the stars after a storm no one saw.

I'm from the camera around my neck and the lens that's become my eyes.

I'm from those times of happiness right before it all fell apart.

I'm from that moment you laid eyes on me,

To that moment you said goodbye to me.

I'm from a God who loves me even when I cannot love myself.

I'm from love and hate and all in between.

I'm from those nights I never thought I
    could survive,
With that cold blade pressed tight against
    my skin.
To those days I never wanted to stop living,
As the sun starts to warm my soul as it rises
    up each morning.
I'm from the deaths that came before me and
    the lives that will come after me.

I'm from more than words can describe in one
    twenty-four-hour day.
I'm from life and death and that simple line
    in between.

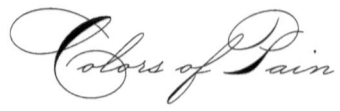
Colors of Pain

It's the dirt-brown feeling in your gut when you know you have failed.

It's the sad gray look in your kids' eyes when they know you are lying about the liquor on your breath.

It's the yellow grit on your teeth after smoking for too many years.

And coming home to a former lover having to say your day was fine.

Even though that's a lie.

It's the red-hot steam on your ears when you walk past a homeless person.

And they look at you with crystal blue eyes,

So full of hope and bright love.

But your dark soul can't spare a second.

It's the black abyss in your mind as you watch a little boy go up to a casket and say goodbye to someone he never had the chance to know.

It's the purple tint on your lips as your lie in bed next to someone each night who could take your life if you said "no."

It's the dark red blood that spills from
   your hand as you write a love note to
   the lady down the street,
And the green sickness in your heart because
   you know she'll never write back.

It's the pale pink words of your forever
   friend's last words,
As you squeeze her hand just a little tighter,
Hoping to keep her grounded to this world.

We use the colors of the rainbow to describe
   the things we love,
The things that make us happy.
But why do we not use these same colors to
   describe the things that make us
   uncomfortable?
That make us sad?
Would we start to accept these terrible
   truths as part of life?
And what is so wrong with that?

Most kids view the color yellow as sunshine
   and happiness,

But what would happen if they knew that the
      color yellow would be the last color
      they saw in the eyes of someone they
      love dying in a hospital bed?

Most kids view green as the color of new
      grass and springtime,

Hope and growth.

But what would happen if they knew that the
      color green would be the color of the
      sickness they feel in the pit of their
      heart when someone they love lies
      to them?

Why do we take the rainbow,

So full of these colors,

And sing all these happy songs?

When the same color that represents love
      also represents hate?

How can we sing that these colors only
      represent joy?

And what is so wrong with the blue of sadness?

All That Is Mine

When my lover asks me, "How are you?"
I want to tell her that I am every bit as happy as the day I lost a three-month old in Zimbabwe.

When she finally talks to me after a long day of silence,
Of 'productivity,'
And asks, "How are you?"
I want to tell her that I am every bit as sad as the day I got into the college program of my dreams.

See,
I don't like that question.
"How are you?"

How am I?
What is that even asking?
How am I emotionally?
God knows no one cares.
How am I the way I am?
God knows I have no clue.
How am I compared to who I used to be?
Maybe that is the question worth answering.

After being broken down by the only person I thought could ever love me,

By the way he was the one who told me that no one else could ever love me.

After being shattered and left on this side of Heaven by the one person I thought would never leave me,

By the way,

She is the one person I apparently knew nothing about.

After drowning in my own depression and thinking I had finally found bliss at the bottom of that dark ocean floor,

Then to have someone yank me out and tell me that I needed to part with that way of life.

And then actually trying to part from it,

All while being told to keep my troubles and pains to myself because no one was going to help me but me.

By the way,

My depression is the only interesting thing about me.

It's the only person who has always stuck around.

Or so it keeps telling me.

I spent my nights in girlhood learning not
    to be picky about foods or colors,
Because God forbid I be a bit different.
I spent my nights in middle school perfecting
    my handwriting,
Page after page of letters and words,
Because God forbid my words be unique,
God forbid I have a quirk,
Or five.

Now the only thing left that is mine,
That is me,
Is my depression.
Though I'm told half the people my age have
    depression so I guess not even that
    is mine.
Maybe nothing is truly mine.

Maybe,
If I started walking,
Off this page,
Out that door,
Across state lines,
Through the ocean.
I would walk right off the edge of the map,

Find people like me.
Those told that being unique is wrong.
That being you is too much.
That I am too much.

People who have experienced life in its
    truest form,
And decided to show life their truest form.
And failed.

But maybe,
Even there,
I wouldn't belong.

I buried my great grandma at twelve.
My aunts at thirteen and sixteen.
My uncles at fourteen and nineteen.
A baby at twenty.
But I still love like I've never known loss.

I had my soul ripped out through my vagina
    at eight.
But I still love like I've never known a
    violent touch.

My heart was stolen at thirteen by a deadbeat
    of a boy,
He returned it to me like ruins of a
    demolished building.
Pieces missing or too heavy to fit back in,
Shredding my still-bleeding chest as I tried.
But I still love like it's the first time
    someone ever told me they loved me.
Like it's the first time I ever told someone
    I loved them.

I tried to cut myself out of existence three
    times before I turned fifteen.
As if the chords tying me to this life were
    mere threads I needed to break free from.
Instead of seeing them as the threads that
    hang my masterpiece of a being from
    the walls of Heaven.
I still love like every human is a masterpiece.

Because maybe,
If I believe that every human is a masterpiece,
Then I'll believe that I am human,
And I am a masterpiece, too.

So maybe living with people on the outskirts
    of a map isn't for me.
Maybe fitting in anywhere isn't for me.

Maybe I'm meant to live here,
With you.
All you loving humans,
Who know nothing about me,
But whose souls now know everything.

And as I continue to look,
I see that the edge of this map never really
    gets closer.
I walk and walk,
But that horizon is always just out of reach.

And my arms no longer want to reach out,
And draw that line in.
They just want to reach out,
And draw you in.
So I can love you with my whole being.
Which is all I have to offer.

And don't worry,
If you leave me,
I will still love with my whole being.
Because that is all that I have.
That is all that is mine.

Dear World

I wish you had told me how hard life would get before it ever got better.
I wish you had told me all the memories I should have been making,
Instead of spending hours agonizing over work that would still be there tomorrow.
I wish you had told me that someone could love me without demanding anything in return.
I wish you had told me that the monsters under my bed would become my only friends.

I wish you had told me that I would be forced to endure this hatred and ridicule every day,
But they would simply call it school and expect me to keep going.
They say, "Stand up for yourself!"
But don't you dare make a scene otherwise,
It's all your fault.

I wish you had told me to love myself before ever loving someone else.
I wish you had told me how simple death is.

Wishes upon stars are simply that:
A hopeful breath given to dead light to
    change the entire world.
What is so romantic about wishes?
About dreams?
About stars?
I wish you had told me.
"I wish I may, I wish I might,"
What is this verse even saying?
We wish for now but we ask for later.
How can we expect that to change anything?
I wish you had told me.

I wish you had told me how precious a single
    smile is,
Before all we could see were frowns.
I wish you had told me how evil cancer is.
I wish you had told me that the color yellow
    is the worst color in the rainbow.
I wish you had told me how much love hurts.

You're not a number you're a name,
But the first time you mess up they won't use your name.
Teachers tell us that family comes first,
But then get upset when you visit grandma in the hospital because today could be her last day and you have to miss a class.
Why is high school so important,
When all it does is teach us the Pythagorean Theorem and how to lose our friends?
I wish you had told me.

I wish you had told me how much destruction words can cause.
They say it's okay to cry but don't do it here
Or there in fact,
Just don't do it.
I wish you had told me how much music heals.

I wish you had told me that magic isn't real and Cinderella is just a fairy tale.
I wish you had told me that there are no happy endings in the real world.

They say we're all princesses but when Prince Charming finally comes we realize he's just a drunk and we wasted our time but hey that's okay!

At least we can say we tried!

I wish you had told me not to spend all that time on my looks.

Because I'm beautiful just the way I am.

But if everyone believed they were beautiful,

Then businesses would run out of money and we have to keep the rich happy.

You're perfect just the way you are but no one is perfect,

So what am I?

Please don't ask me what I am because I don't know and I don't want to know.

I wish you had told me why we tell our children to dream big,

But when they grow up we tell them to keep their feet on the ground,

Because a head in the clouds can't possibly put food on the table.

I wish you had told me why we have to keep the rich so happy,

When the happiest people in the world can be found on the streets.

Because they know life isn't about how many things we can fill a house with.

It's about how many memories we can fill our hearts with.

Why is that not taught in schools?

I wish you had told me.

I wish you had told me why it's so important to be popular in a world,

Where we will always be hated by someone.

Why do we define others by what they like to do,

But then call them lame when we don't agree?

I wish you had told me why it's okay for you to tell someone to kill themself,

But no one dare say that to your best friend.

Why don't we stand up for the odd girl who sits alone at lunch?

I wish you had told me why we spend more
    time teaching girls what they can and
    cannot wear to prevent rape,
Instead of teaching people to just not rape!
Why do we worry about our children doing
    something they love but could get
    them bullied,
Instead of teaching everybody to just love?
Love goes so much further than hate,
But we don't actually believe that,
We just tell it to people so they feel better.
I wish you had told me why we have to worry
    about how others view us,
When the only opinion that really matters
    is God's.

Why do people think they can't be saved on
    their death bed?
I wish you had told me that God will always
    love me even when I mess up,
Instead of just waiting for me to figure
    that out on my own.

I wish you had listened to me when I said
    I wasn't okay,
Instead of just telling me that life will
    get better if I just give it time.
Not everything will be okay,
And that's okay.

God has a plan,
But if you ask a preacher about hardships,
They will simply say,
"God will bring you through it."
Did God really plan for His children to be
    in so much pain?
I wish you had told me.

People talk about God and forget about the Devil.
As if not talking about him will make him
    not exist.
I wish you had told me the Devil is real
    before I laid in his bed.

It Rained Last Night

It rained last night.

Not the kind of rain that goes pitter-patter on your roof and feels like kisses from heaven on your skin.

It rained like the heavens had been keeping a secret for far too long,

And could no longer hold it in.

And I knew what that secret was.

Did you?

My secret was that I dipped my toes back into the pool of self-harm after three years of being clean because I missed that feeling of control.

What was your secret?

Did the rain let it all go, too?

Or is there going to be another storm?

If so please let me know,

I'll wear my swimsuit all day just waiting,

Waiting for the heavens to break open and pour out more secrets.

More of our secrets.

Maybe the secret is that heaven is just too small,
Just too lonely,
So all the angels cry out when it becomes too much to bear.
And the thunder is god yelling back,
Yelling at them to act normal.
For heaven's sake,
Act normal,
Like we're supposed to.
Act like heaven is everything we believed it to be while on earth.

Maybe heaven isn't the greatest destination after all.
Maybe we have no destination.
Just an endless journey of sunshine as happiness,
And rain as tears.
With someone always yelling for us to change,
For us to be better.
To be good enough,
Like we were taught to be.

All I want in this life is for someone to tell me that I am good enough.

That I am good.

And enough.

At this point I don't even care if it's god or a dog I pass on the street.

Just let me be enough.

Just me.

Let all my secrets come pouring down,

Like the way it rained last night.

Let all my tears come flowing down,

Like the way it rained last night.

And let one person,

Just one person,

Stand outside for hours,

Just watching my storm.

Let them smile when my tears get too heavy and start to chill their skin.

Let them laugh when my screams roll too loud and they can feel it in their chest.

And let them be amazed at the way my heart lights up the night sky as my passions set it on fire.

I want someone to watch my storms,
The way I watched it rain last night.
No thought that it should stop.
No thought of ways to make it change.
No fear of being hurt.
Just wonder.
Just amazement.
Just,
Enough.

Dear Quiet Renaissance Man

When I first met you,

My heart fluttered back to that of a twelve-year-old girl.

A young girl who reads her horoscope like she's supposed to read the Bible.

And who compares her Zodiac sign to yours to see if the stars will line up.

Lucky for us,

It's the year of the Eclipse.

My mind drifted off to a far-off land,

Where I still believed in Princes and fairy tales

And the chance to plan my own wedding like all the other little girls I knew.

I love the story about Humans.

The one where Zeus made us with two heads and four arms and four legs.

But then,

He felt threatened by us so he split us into two and my soul continues to fly to yours as if begging you to be my other half.

But you were too busy worrying about financial stability,

You didn't have time to even believe in souls.

Where did the stars go wrong?

Maybe it's because you grew up
With Jesus and family suppers,
And I grew up learning
If you want to hurt someone then you slash
    three of their tires instead of four.
Because insurance companies believe if
    you're not
Fully
Broken,
Then you must
Not
Be broken.
I think this really speaks about our society today.
If we aren't,
Fully
Broken bodies,
Then we must
Not
Be broken.

If I just

Lost my job but I still have my house then
    I must

Not

Be broken.

If I just

Lost my dog but I still have my children
    then I must

Not

Be broken.

If I just

Have a few scars on my wrist

But I'm not hooked up to an IV drip and
    overdosing on Morphine then I must

Not

Be broken.

Quiet Renaissance Man,
You are the best thing that
Almost
Happened to me.
But since you didn't
Fully
Happen to me,
I guess none of this matters.

It's like
We're playing chess but,
The colors are all wrong and
You're playing with your mind while I'm
Playing with my heart and . . .
Why do we keep doing this??
Why don't we just crash into each other like stars?
Who cares if we cause a black hole.
Let the whole world watch!

But,
Quiet Renaissance Man,
Are you even,
A Renaissance Man?
You don't
Open the car door for me.
You don't
Walk me to my car at night.
Quiet Renaissance Man,
You don't
Even hold my hand.

Maybe it's just me but,
Are you even a Renaissance Man?
Or is this just one
Big Lie?
And if so,
Who are you trying to fool?
Me?
Or you?

My Giant

For six months,

I've stared at that dull brown painted brick wall which isolates this house from all the rest.

Isolates this building of four walls and a roof and a god-awful stove intent on burning every meal we cook.

I stare at this wall and the green giant slumped over it.

As if having just come from a battle and is too exhausted to lift its head.

This giant has fingers that drape over the painted brick wall with such gentleness,

Caressing each bump and crack in the paint.

As if telling the wall that it knows what lies beneath,

And still loves it.

During the day as the sun comes up over my giant,

As the wind starts to rustle the leaves that have become like hair,

My sleepy giant comes to life.

I hear him whisper,

I like to think to me.

Some days,
He likes to sleep in and just bask in the
    warmth the sun brings.
Other days I can hear him whispering even
    before dawn.
Maybe begging for a lost love to return,
Or for a small bird to land on its branch the
    way a butterfly lands on human skin.

I wonder if my giant can feel like I do.
If not,
Does he want to?
Does he crave the ability to walk away
    from this painted brick wall
And all his battles to simply see the
    world as his own?

If my giant had feet to run away,
Would he ever come back?
What would keep him here?
That painted brick wall just stands there,
Offering no affection in return.

I sit,
Watching my giant take in the morning glory.
I see him start to come to life.
I hear him start to whisper,
Maybe even sing.

How many secrets does my giant hold?
How many memories and lives has he seen walk past his eyes?
How many have cared to look back into his?

Can he smell my coffee? I added cinnamon.
I wonder if he knows what that tastes like.

Has he ever had the pleasure of decorating for Christmas?
Ornaments hung by his delicate and strong fingers,
Knowing not to let a single one break.
Lights strung up around his body brighter than the light of the moon he falls asleep to each night.
The sound of Christmas music flowing through his leafy hair.

I see him stirring,
Bringing every leaf and branch to life just
　　　as I would,
My fingers and toes coming out of a deep sleep.
What are his plans for today?
Who is he going to battle?
Will he win?

Dear Fear

I'll start nice.
It's good to see you.
Sometimes,
I feel like you try to hide,
But you still want to be in my life.
After all,
You are part of me,
And I want to love you.
Truly.

But we need to talk.
Girl,
What is goin' on?
I'm not sure you even know what you're doing to me at times.
Do you know how fast my heart has been beating?
Do you know how many nights I've laid in bed not sleeping?
My mind racing and my body tense from everything inside me?

What is all that for?
I want to accept you,
To love you,
To give you space.

But I can't have you diminishing the space I
    am allowed to take up.

What is it you need?
What can I do to love you today?
Is it acknowledgment?
Is it the fact you hate it when I try to act
    like you don't exist?
I get that.

Okay home girl.
This is your space.
You can speak.
You can yell.
You can cry.
You can shake.

You.
Can.
Exist.

I know you are real.
You are part of me,
And that is okay.
That is good.

We can get to all our finish lines together.

I'll hold your hand,
And you'll hold mine.
We'll make this the greatest love story ever told.

I know you don't mean to keep me away from love.
I know it's not all your fault.
People lie.
People leave.
You simply don't want that for me.
And I appreciate you for that.

But this is one of those times where you can't try to make me shrink and take up less space than I deserve.
I am giving you space to fully exist.
Now you need to give me space to fully exist.
Deal?
Good.

Now take my hand.
We have a finish line to cross.

The End

So there you have it,
My friend or foe.
My life story written out in poetry,
Squished between these pages.
Bound up for your consumption.

How do you feel?
What did you feel?
Did you learn anything?
I would love for these words to have transcended
    these pages into your heart and soul.
Showing you,
To love yourself.
Showing you,
That you are worthy of so much more.
Capable,
Of so much more.

Please don't focus on me.
Please don't let this be just "my" story.
Let these words be that explosion which
    propels you into the next chapter.
And let that chapter be you,
Telling your own story.
Telling your own truths.

I wrote this all down because I needed to heal.
I still need to heal.
And don't we all?
Don't you?
Let this be your blanket permission slip allowing yourself to go after your own healing relentlessly.
Chase it down and grab hold,
Knowing that you have the power of the whole universe within you.

You don't need three clicks of some ruby-red heels.
Or the fitting of a glass slipper.
Or the rubbing of a lamp.
You just need to grab hold of the power inside you,
And know fully that you house the entire cosmos within your soul.

Don't believe me?
Even science says we are formed from the same material as stars.

You are an entire galaxy.
Honor that in yourself.

We are each entire galaxies.
Honor that in others.

I am an entire galaxy, I honor that in myself.

I honor that in you.

And with that,
I leave you,
To your own entire infinite cosmos.

Copyright © 2020 by Keelia Trively

All rights reserved. This book or any portion thereof may not be reproduced or used in any manner whatsoever without the express written permission of the author except for brief quotations in a book review.

About the Author

This is me. I started writing poetry in second grade, in a notebook I made from a Frosted Flakes cereal box. It was the first creative outlet I delved into, and I have dreamed of publishing it ever since.

It's taken many years, a few different countries, and moving to a new state to finally make this dream come true.

Thank you for joining this journey, and thank you for allowing me to be part of yours.

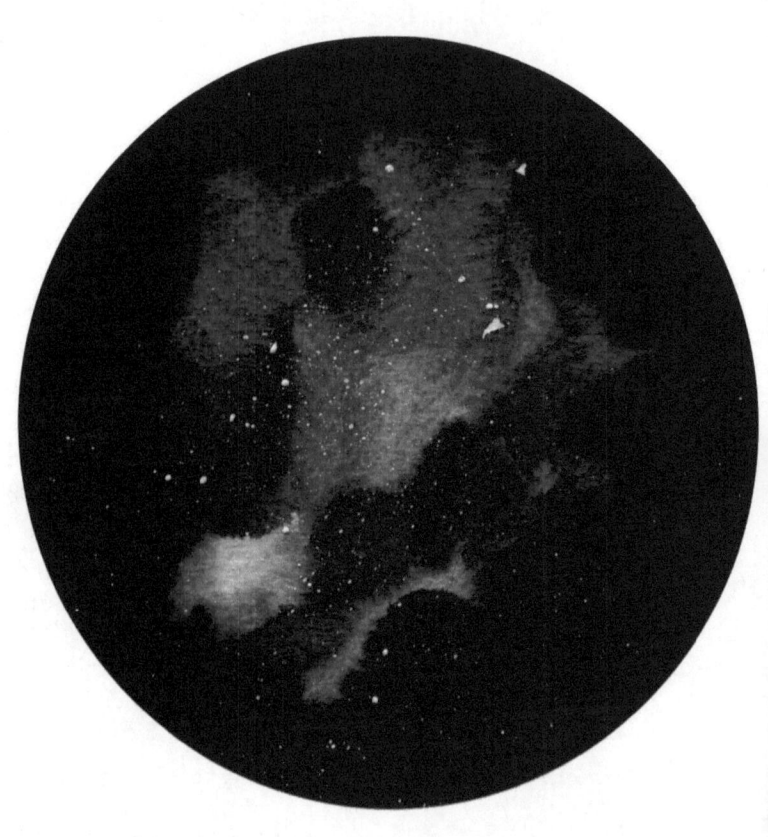